This Tangled Web

I0118159

Kate Swift

chipmunkapublishing
the mental health publisher

Kate Swift

Published by
Chipmunkapublishing
PO Box 6872
Brentwood
Essex CM13 1ZT
United Kingdom

http://www.chipmunkapublishing.com

Edited by Aleks Lech

Chipmunkapublishing gratefully acknowledge the support of Arts Council England.

ARTS COUNCIL ENGLAND

Foreword

I feel extremely honoured to have this opportunity to make this introductory contribution to this exceptional book by Kate. I was her therapist for a number of years, and together we went on an extremely difficult journey to help her move from victim to survivor. It is so quick and easy to write "victim to survivor" but the emotional journey was long and hard, and anything but easy!

Physical,emotional and sexual abuse in childhood profoundly damages the child's sense of self and denies them the opportunity to get some or all of their core needs met. As Kate describes, when very young, she needed to hide under the table to escape from the rantings of her drunken father to find the sense of safety that she had a right to expect both her parents to provide. When the sexual abuse started she tried to give signals that something was wrong, but the dysfunctional nature of the family resulted in her need for protection being ignored or missed. A dependent and developing child trying to make sense of an abusive environment will often erroneously blame themselves for the abuse they are experiencing or needs not being responded to or met, rather than attribute the blame to the abuser or carer. This can then lay the foundations for the development of problems that may not fully surface until the victim reaches adulthood and attempts independence.

Very early on in our work together, Kate started giving me poetry and writing that she had either written before we met or in response to one or more of our sessions. At this stage of her therapy it was often easier for her to communicate through her writing, rather than voice it in the session. I was immediately struck by the power of her work and often moved by it. I remember on many occasions suggesting to Kate that I thought she ought to share it with others, as it could perhaps encourage others who had been abused start or continue on their journey towards that of survivor.

Kate's writing and drawing became an integral part of her therapy, so it is with immense pleasure that I heard she had been given this opportunity to share her work with others. It is a sign of just how far she has come that she has been able to put together a website(all her own work) and now present this book. Her story gives hope that no matter what the nature of the abuse, it is possible to survive and have a life beyond it.

Christopher Moore MSc
Schema Therapist (ISST)
Cognitive-behavioural Psychotherapist (BABCP)

Note: For those who may be interested, the therapy approach we used was called Schema Focused Therapy (SFT), an approach developed by Dr Jefferey E Young over the past 25 years and now developing a growing evidence base for its efficacy.

I hope one day that survivors of Childhood Sexual Abuse will no longer be silenced. As we join our voices together, we will become so loud that we will never be able to be shunned or silenced again. It is time for the Phoenix in all of us to rise from the ash pile.

A collection of poetry and art on the subject of childhood sexual abuse written by the person who lived it and who now lives after it...the web is no longer so tangled and I certainly am not trapped by it. These poems are now yours to help you on your own journey. I am not totally 'fixed' but I am no longer totally broken.

This Tangled Web

Given the subject matter, a lot of the poems within the following pages may be distressing. I have shared almost everything about my own experience. I was tempted to not include some pieces because they are still quite raw for me, but I wanted to share as much as possible. I didn't want to hold anything back that someone else may be able to identify with. It is important to look after yourself...maybe just read one every now and then when you feel you want and need to...maybe read a few when you feel strong and have good support available to you. I want these poems to be a tool to help you...please read them with care for yourself.

Thank You
I want to dedicate this book to my Psychologist Christopher Moore for helping me to unravel and make sense of my childhood. I will never as long as I live forget what you did for me and my inner child.

I also want to acknowledge and thank a few very close friends who walked this journey with me and to all the amazing survivors I am meeting through 'Tangled Web'.

Kate Swift

CHAPTER ONE...THE ABUSE AND ABUSER

A silent movie inside my head...

I was abused by a sibling for almost half of my childhood years. It began when I was 8 and he is just a few years older than me. Sometimes I really fought hard to not let him do it to me and sometimes I was tired and scared, I just let him win. When I told I was rejected by family and he was protected by family. One parent said "I believe it happened but it's not as bad as she said it was". I was fostered for 6 months and told I had more friends, I was stronger and he needed her. I saw several counselors and therapists before I found the one who was right for me. I told because I actually feared I was carrying 'his' child...thank God I wasn't, but those weeks when I thought I could be were hell on earth. Nobody around me talked about what happened and I tried to make sense of it and get some feelings out initially through writing...writing these poems and just writing how I felt. I always wanted these poems to be used for good some day and I hope this is the day. I also read as much about the subject as I could get my hands on...I needed something to identify with...I needed to not feel so alone. For anyone wondering what happened to 'him' when it all came to light...he said he abused me because he had been assaulted by someone else before...of course that is awful and should not have happened to him but we have to stop allowing people to use that as a reason to go on and inflict damage. There are countless adults in this world who were abused as children and who go on to be wonderful, safe, caring adults...he was eventually given a police caution (because he had previously suffered himself!!!) and I was told he had done some therapy and was safe to be around...he was not safe to be around. When are we going to go all out to protect our children rather than going all out to protect *those who abuse?*

~

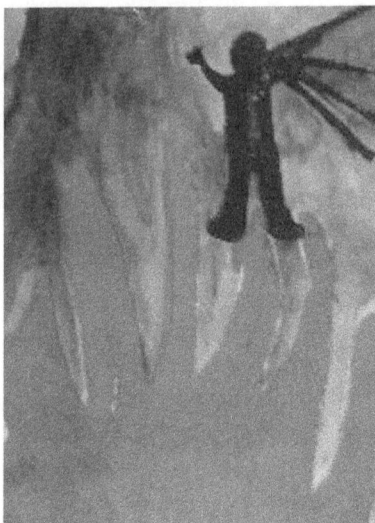

See the child half clothed on the floor
He did it to her and he has done it many times before
See the child awake and so afraid in the night
Because he would come and pin her down so tight.
See the child crying herself to sleep again
He does not care for her feelings, she is drenched in
pain
See the child wondering if she holds within her another
life
She wants to die...tablets...razor blades...a knife.
See the child who is battered and bruised
With the invisible scars of the abused
See the child who once was a babe in her mother's arm
How did she come to so much harm?

~

THE RAG DOLL AND THE PRINCESS

She is his object, a play thing and nothing more
She is his rag doll to pull around and then dump on the floor
She is a something until he takes what he wants, takes it all
She is his rag doll, set up to fall.
She is a means to an end, there for his taking
She is his rag doll from a nightmare never waking
She is his filthy, squalid secret, one never to tell
She is his rag doll trapped inside hell.
The rag doll wants to be a princess one day
To be rescued from hell and taken far away
To be given a new dress untouched by him
To be sterilized from all his filth and sin;
To be innocent and to be sweet
To feel like a princess, all lovely and complete
To be seen as something more than a rag doll
To be un-abused, un-touched and gloriously whole.

~

~

When you abused me you placed a silent movie in my head
That I have seen so many times whilst trying to sleep in my bed.
When you touched me you left a permanent imprint on my skin
Flooded with fear and pain whilst remembering.
When you held my wrists so I could not get away
You captured a little girl who remains captured to this very day.
When I think too much and when the floorboards creak
I still feel the dread and fail to sleep
The way you looked at me with sleepy eyes
I remember it all so completely and yet it is me I despise.

~

Night time was when HE came
When he left me in pain
When I felt so much fear in my home
When I never wanted to be alone
When nightmares filled my mind
When the world was so unkind
When I longed for the day
To come and wash my tears away.

~

He stands up and pulls his trousers back up to his waist
He is rushing out the door in silent haste
She is left behind, a heap on the floor
He walks across the landing closing the door
Her body is hurting where he touched her so forcefully
She wonders how long he will leave her be
She feels like rubbish, used and thrown away
& WHY is the question she can never make her mouth say.

~

This Tangled Web

You are forcing yourself onto me
I feel I am at your mercy
Suffocating under the weight of you
Ashamed by what you force me to do
Hemmed in your twisted desire
It is me that gets caught in the fire
I am kissed, touched, held down, raped in body and
innocence
I am so confused that nothing is making sense
I am left alone
Feeling more pain than I have ever known
Now I meet face to face with shame
As it becomes the essence of my name.
~

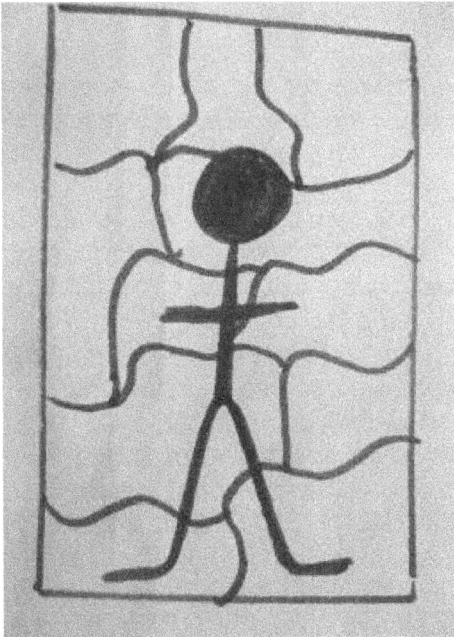

~
I see before me a child paralyzed by fear
Screaming a scream no one will hear
She is bewildered and semi-naked on the floor

Torn are the clothes she wore
I see the confusion in her face
I see a violation in that place
She is crying, crying alone
She has been violated in her home
I see eyes cast down to the floor in shame
I see arms an angry shade of red in pain
I see a child withdrawing into her shell
I see before me a piece of hell.

~

Is he going to come to my room tonight?
Pull the quilt up close and leave on the light
The floor boards creak and I feel the fear
Every little sound rings in my ear
I pray it is not tonight, or if it is it won't be for long
Before he has been and gone
And left me once again wondering why
And left me once again wanting to die.

~

INSIDE THE BOY
When you placed your hand on me, what was I to you?
When did you plan what you would do?
How did it feel when you gripped me tight?
How did it feel creeping around at night?
How did a monster come from a boy?
When did I become your property, a toy?
How did you justify what you did?
Did you not see in front of you a little kid?

~

I want to know what it feels like to be free
To have no memory of what you did to me
The only way to freedom is to cut away the pain
Yet it always finds its way back to me again
I hate myself and I feel sick inside
From you, why can't I hide?
I'm so angry with you but I just cry useless tears
You have cursed so many of my years

This Tangled Web

I wish someone else could feel the way I do...
Then they would understand what it is like to remember
you.
~
The weak in the hands of the strong
By mental and physical strength they do wrong
The little girl is silenced by fear
She is screaming in terror, a scream only she can hear
He is hurting her, holding her wrist real tight
But his crimes are covered by the blanket of night
He looks at her and she know what he expects her to do
Like an animal caught in a trap she has to see it through
She can feel him but she is not there
Her mind is counting patterns on the wallpaper, or
anywhere
That is the tyranny of the strong
By mental and physical strength they do wrong.
~
Every room holds a memory of you
The place where I sleep still seems haunted too
I can still feel your hands all over me
The look that told me I was not free
Questions I wanted to ask rattle around in my mind
I am caught in memories that bind
My soul has been dented, where can I find peace?
How can I be free of you?...give me some release.
~
Sometimes my life is hell
I carry so many burdens that I cannot tell
I feel torn apart inside
Part of me seems to have died
BECAUSE OF YOU
Some days I feel like total rubbish
I wonder how my life came to this
I cut to take the inner pain away
It takes all my energy to get through the day

BECAUSE OF YOU
Each morning I wake up and take a pill
Force myself to function against my will
Often I cry on my own
In a room full of people I can feel totally alone
BECAUSE OF YOU
During the night I lay awake in fear
Even though I know you are not here
I remember things I want to forget
I am stung with shame and regret
BECAUSE OF YOU
I look in the mirror and I hate what I see
I feel so trapped and yet I want to be free
Finding it hard to relax and to rest
Always feeling I can never be more than 2nd best
BECAUSE OF YOU.

~

You raped me
You raped my little girl
You raped my childhood
You raped my memories
You raped my past
You raped my today
You rape my tomorrow
You raped me of myself
You raped my of normality
You raped me of peace of mind
You raped me of restful sleep
You raped my inner child
You raped me.

~

YOU
You make me feel sick inside
You make me want to curl up and hide
You make me feel afraid and alone
You make me feel unknown
You make me feel like the worst thing on earth

This Tangled Web

You make me feel like I have no worth
You make me feel like I was a mistake
You make me feel like I was yours to take
You make me feel angry...calm but angry
You make me feel like I am not free
You make me want to draw blood from my skin
You make me feel the need to cleanse from within
You make me feel sick inside
You make me feel like a part of me died.

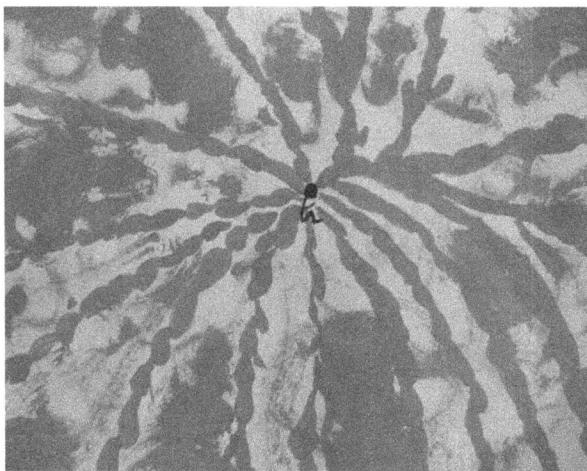

~

WHEN THE MORNING COMES
In the dark of the night she is asleep in her bed
Stuffed toys around her, one beside her head
Her school books scattered on the floor
Teen idol posters blue tacked to the door
In the dark of the night she is woken from her sleep
Woken by someone's twisted desire that will not keep
Her school books scattered on the floor
Beside the nightshirt which he tore
Stuffed toys around her, one beside her head
As she sobs into her pillow and wishes she was dead
When the morning comes she is a child again

She dresses in her school uniform and buries the pain.

~

The poison you injected me with aged eight
When you abused me and sealed my fate
It courses through my veins to this very day
I don't think it will ever fully go away
It is like a dirty stain that I can never clean
A dirty, cheap, squalid feeling mostly unseen
Sometimes it hits me like a punch in the face
& I feel like the lowest object in the place
Why did you ever lay your hand on me?
Why couldn't my little girl be free?
I would give anything to be clean again
To feel normal; free; sane.

~

The scars you gave me I carry everywhere
The haunting chill of your stare
My childhood snatched away
Through abuse, not innocent play
A human doll, picked up and thrown back down again
Pinned down by the past, crippled with emotional pain
I was a puppet and he held the strings
I watch children at play so carefree
I cannot say it was like that for me.

~

PICTURES & PRETENCE
I look at the photo; you were raping me back then
It is a school photo and I was nine or ten
I guess you would say a typical girl like any other
Your average family, sister and brother
Yet nothing in my life was average in your hands
Much of my time was about you and your demands
Just a child in a photo...
Guess they'll never know.

~

This Tangled Web

~

Mummy mummy he is coming I need you to rescue me
Mummy mummy where are you I need you now to help
me
Mummy mummy his sleepy eyes are scary, my
nightshirt is torn
Mummy mummy hold me in your arms, every part of me
hurts
Mummy mummy can you hear me calling out your
name?
Mummy mummy wash away my shame
Mummy mummy where are you, I feel so alone
Mummy mummy, guess I am on my own.

~

Thinking about what you did feels like it's happening all
over again
Like my wrists are pinned down and I am locked in your
repulsive game
It's like you are here and I am a child once more
You held me against the wall; you pulled me to the floor
& suddenly this place does not feel like home
& suddenly I don't want to be alone

*It's like any second now you will walk in the door and
over to me
From this hell in my mind, let me be free
Every tiny sound in the house is ringing in my ears
Everything is back again, all that I feared
Thinking about what you did to me feels like it's
happening all over again
So real are the memories, so fresh is the pain.*

~

*Brother mine I beg you to let me go free
Why me, why me?
Brother mine don't...please don't touch me there
Don't pull off my clothing and leave me bare
Brother mine you know this is wrong
You are hurting me; your grip is too strong
Brother mine please, please don't force my hand
I don't, I cannot understand
Brother mine you leave me in pain
Please don't do it to me again
Brother mine in my mind are what if and why
When you have finished I can do nothing but cry
Brother mine I was your little sister, a child like any other
Now I am little more than nothing and you cannot be my
brother.*

~

*THE FIGURE IN THE NIGHT
All my dignity you stole away from me
The signs people failed to see
You pulled me around, your grip so tight
Haunted by you each night
Pinned up against the wall, I was his fool
I now wake in the night and gaze at the ceiling
My dreams are haunting and causing bad feeling
Will the torment end?
Will my battered heart mend?
The dream closes in around me
The touch of you strong in my memory*

This Tangled Web

Your hands all over me, the panic inside making me choke
A figure in the night, the darkness for a cloak
His body forced upon mine
Cold shivers down my spine
I can feel his breath
I want death
My wrists are finger marked
My body aching
My soul is on fire
My child sized heart breaking.

~

AFTER ABUSE
My innocence gone
My soul bruised
My laughter shadowed
My pain increased
My fear intensified
My trust broken...
A part of me gone forever.

~

Did you hear me say NO, did you feel me resist you?
Did your memory fail you when you said it wasn't true?
I feel sick when I remember, I feel like that girl all over again
I want to cut myself to feel a different kind of pain
One that I can live with more easily...
Whilst walking to the day when I am free.

~

I want you to know there is no reason or excuse
To make me forgive abuse
To make me forget or feel sorry for you
It has been hell through and through
Stolen innocence, a thief in the night
Nothing can ever make what you did all right.

~

BEING EIGHT
He did what he did - I was eight
He came into my bed - I was alone
I told him no - he ignored me
I pushed him away - he persisted
I wanted to ask why - I was silent
He used me - I was his rag doll
He had control - I was eight.

~

Like an invisible wall you trap me
Like an invisible hand you pin me down
Like a silent voice you frighten me
Like a robot you control me...
GIVE MY LIFE BACK TO ME.

~

I've been robbed
HELP
POLICE
Call 999
Stolen my innocence
My childhood time
He has taken everything
I am empty inside
Lock him away
Give me the key
Get him
Catch him
Don't let him go
Tell him he is a bad bad boy
Tell him I am not his toy
I've been robbed
HELP
POLICE
Call 999

~

When he came and placed his hands on me
My innocence forever gone, never again can it be

This Tangled Web

He raped me and I can never reverse what he did
It is the day I stopped being just like any other kid
When he kissed my neck and forced my hand
I had to be a grown up and try to understand
My skin carries his touch and I cannot wash it away
He chose to abuse me and I have to pay.

~

I am not here, you cannot hurt me again
I am not living therefore I do not feel pain
I have taken myself away from you
I have taken the little girl away from what you put her through
You cannot reach me no matter how hard you try
She has no need to feel afraid or to cry
You cannot control her any more, you have not won
You will not find me under this sun
I finally have control
You cannot rape, damage or abuse my soul.

~

CHAPTER TWO…Telling/The disclosure

How can I tell you…?

All I can say about the time of my disclosure is that I hope things have changed a lot in the years since then. I would not want any child to have the case treated in some of the ways mine was. I feel I was failed by different people on different levels at a time when you need those people the most. I only told because I felt totally trapped and could see no other way out, otherwise maybe I would never have told, I cannot know.

This Tangled Web

I tried to tell you in a language without words
Tried to show you what was happening to me
Tried to open your eyes and willed you to see
To come and rescue an eight year old from the pit of
abuse
From something I did not control or choose
For you to restore to me what was rightfully mine
I grieve for my childhood; you only get one in a lifetime
I wanted you to save me, to be strong
To protect me furiously and assure me he was wrong
To stop him abusing me year after year
I screamed so many silent screams...
Why didn't you hear?

~

I wish I was talking about the weather, current affairs or
anything
Not about what he did to me, I don't know how to talk
about him
I wish I could just tell you and not feel the fear and pain
I wish I could look you in the eye but I am crippled with
the shame
I think so little of me therefore you would think it too
You might smile and say the opposite but I know what is
really true
If only I could tell the secrets of my soul
It would break his grip on me and I could at last be
whole.

~

DISCLOSURE
H-ow can I tell you what he is doing to me, I can't
E-xcept in ways without words
L-isten, why won't you listen to my silent plea?
P-lease I want him to stop, make him stop

M-y mind is in agony trying to work out what to do

E-asy, no it is virtually impossible to have to tell

P-eople, all these people that now know, I am ashamed
L-iar, he is twisting the truth
E-motionally I am so exhausted
A-ngry, confused, torn apart inside
S-he is making me leave, does not want me any more
E-ating me up inside is the thought of him still with her

A-ll I wanted was for him to stop
N-obody can understand me, nobody
Y-ou say it is for my own good these case conferences
and meetings
O-nly I cannot tell you what I want
N-obody listens to me, nobody
E-verything is out now and worse than ever.

~

~

NO ENTRY
Please don't open up that room
For it will always be too soon
If only you could hear its tormenting sound
Protect me, save me or I will drown

This Tangled Web

Shut the door and lock it tight
Then I am safe from the wounds of the night
Saved from being in his hands again
Sheltered from the pain
The wounds are always raw and the shadows always
fall
I can face nothing and I can face it all.
~
I ASK OF YOU...
I want you to hate him, to show your disgrace
To shout and scream, to forbid him from this place
I want you to ask him and demand to know why
I want you to shatter his every lie
I want him to tell you what he did, so you know
Everything, everything I cannot tell or show
I want you to be sad for your child, for me
I want you to help me be free
I want you to tell me you love me to my face
To hold me secure in this tainted place
I want you to tell me I am not to blame and mean every
word
To listen to my hell and give me the courage to be heard
I want you to have the courage to walk the wilderness of
healing
To face everything you and I are feeling
To stare it in the face until all fear is gone
To be courageous enough to dare to move on
Most of all I want you to love me like you did once upon
a time
If you love me you will rid me of his crime.
~

~

BREAKING THE SILENCE
Who will believe me, who will listen if I tell?
They cannot understand and I want to hide inside a
shell
The thought of a life inside me makes me feel so wild
I could not be a mother to his child
What will happen to me, what will happen to him?
Whichever why I turn it all looks so grim
Surely it's my fault, my own stupidity
The only person to blame is me
If only they know it wouldn't be a secret any more
But it is hidden away behind a locked door
I want to ask him why
I want someone to hold me when I cry
I cannot tell, not today
Tomorrow, yes tomorrow I will tell
I wonder if tomorrow really will be the day I
break the silence?

~

This Tangled Web

Mothers to be and mothers with babies in their care
Looking at the school girl waiting there
In the place of joy and motherhood
Trying to accept the prospect of a baby, no she never could
All adults but for the girl in that place before her time
Foolish girl so they think, knowing nothing of his crime
& you have probably never felt shame like it in your life
The looks that cut her bleeding heart with an assuming knife
Why was she there in school uniform with the babes and mothers to be?
Her years of abuse, violation and rape they did not see
Still she was so cheap in their eyes
Yet she is just a babe herself for who self respect and dignity dies.

~

I stood before you
Your daughter
Abused
Scared

Broken
Torn

Confused

I stood before you

You looked at me and said

I cannot hug you

But you sat and hugged my abusers shirt instead.

~

CHAPTER 3...Family Denial

Mamma make it right...

The subject of abuse disclosure within families and denial is well documented. In my own family I was the outcast, the one to betray her parents by 'telling' someone other than them first. It is still not spoken about years after the disclosure and fine actors would be proud of the Oscar winning performances when we do all meet. I was told to fix the problem I had created by telling, I was also put into care for a time. This website is my way of refusing to be silent. I would write all my feelings down on paper since I was a teenager. Many are the poems you see today, I always wanted them to be used for good. Over a long period of time I learnt to love my family for who they are and not for who and how I want them to be. That does not mean I have forgiven and forgotten, I still don't know that I can ever do that. I guess the poems on this page are a wonderful example of how NOT to react to a disclosure of abuse.

This Tangled Web

Did you just not see?
See what he was doing to me?
Or did you choose to shut your eyes
To protect yourself from pain
Was it easier to believe the lies?
Or was I such a bad girl?
Did you not love me so?
That you knew but chose not to know?
Why didn't you rescue me?
Wasn't I worth it to you?
Surely you knew
~

Today I don't feel like a grown up
Today it hurts so much inside
Today the space between us feels so wide
Today I need you
Today I want to be small again
Today I want to be a child in her mother's care
Today the only place I want to be is there.
~

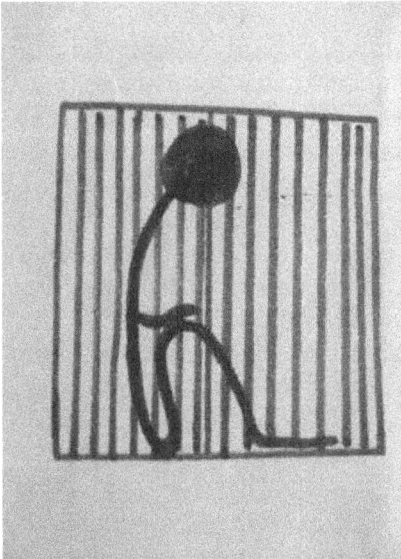

~

Mummy I'm not complete any more
He took my innocence right there on the floor
Mummy I wasn't a little girl from that moment on
Since he did things that were so wrong
Mummy where were you when I cried in shame
When I cringed in pain
Mummy I guess I really am bad just like you taught me
Now I find myself in chains, do I deserve to go free?

~

"I clothed and fed you didn't I?"
That is my mother's battle cry
Like it was everything and such a chore
Like a child should be eternally grateful
& never expect more
You fed my growing body but you starved my heart
You gave me the scraps of your time and often fell apart
You were always too stressed, too tired or too busy
For the little girl who needed to be told you loved me
Emotionally starved within an inch of my heart's will to
live
Maybe you did your best, gave all that you had to give
You clothed my body but not my soul
You left that naked and scarred...
Battered and longing to feel whole
You left me in a wilderness
Where the rag doll wanted to become your princess
Where my soul was confused and lost
Exposed to the elements and now I pay the cost
"I clothed and fed you didn't I?"
You clothed and fed my physical body and you left my
Heart naked...hungry...bone dry.

~

Screaming a silent scream
Come and rescue me mummy
Rape, he raped me mummy
Enter my world, I need you so much

This Tangled Web

Angry mummy, why are you so angry with me?
My mind is so confused
I don't understand any of this
I need you to be the grown up
Give me back some dignity.

~

CHOICES
I didn't choose to be abused
To be held down
To be used
To be forced
To be raped
But you chose to blame me
To reject me
To be angry
To not accept the truth
To abandon me
Am I proud of my choices?
I didn't have any choices
Are you proud of yours?

~

He raped me when I was fifteen and my mother never
came
When she knew, she looked through me like she didn't
know my name
I held the tablets in my hand and thought about what to
do
She told me not to complain, to keep smiling through
I wept on the floor with a heart that was breaking
& she told me all her patience I was taking
When they called a meeting she asked me what to say
and do
To me to pull my family through
Told me to say something to make it right that day
She wanted me to show her the way.

~

FATAL FAILURE

Why weren't you there for me the day he came?
Why weren't you there for me when I wept in shame?
How could you be so remote and blind to it year after year?
Why didn't you stop him and rescue me?
Why didn't through all my nightmares and tears you see?
I feel so angry with you; you left me to be abused
You were only a few minutes away
You failed me back then and you continue to fail me to this day.

~

When I was just a little girl
I could not see the empty well
But now I am grown
Almost ready for children of my own
I understand no water for me
Now I know, now I see
How foolish to seek from a source bone dry
Foolish to will for or to cry
Far better to fill my own full/overflowing
& give abundantly to my children
Whilst they are growing.

~

House of sickness, secrets and lies
You and your people I despise
If the walls could talk what a tale to tell
All you are now is a piece of hell
House of sorrow, sadness and misery
How cruel you are in my memory
You have helped to keep me ill
You do not care how I feel
House of anger, rage and bitterness
Why was I born into this?
The walls are tarnished with discontent

This Tangled Web

Love and understanding long ago spent
House of my childhood
You seem to have never understood
What is really needed to make a home?
I don't want or need you any more
Leave me alone.

~

Take me back into your arms and let me be a child
again
Soothe me in your magical love and dissolve the pain
Look at me and smile; tell me it will be okay
Let me be a child again, if only for one day
Let me live a day without any cares at all
Let me live a day where you will mend me if I fall.

~

Mother embraces your child in pain
Won't you soothe her shame?
Hush your angry heart
Abuse has torn her apart
I know you are hurting but she needs you
To hold her whilst she is sad and blue
Seeing your pain increases her own
She feels so alone
She is still your little girl if you will let her be
Won't you help her to be free?

~

Mummy can you hold my hand?
Can you try to understand?
Can you tell me I am a good girl?
For then my heart would whirl
Can you brush my long brown hair?
Then I will feel like you care
Can you be close when I'm tucked up in bed?
Happy safe thoughts can fill my head
Can you hold me tight and never let me go?
Why do we have to grow?

~

Please don't hurt me any more
Your rejection is a slamming door
I am so tired of feeling the way I do
I'm sick and tired of being hurt by you
If you don't want to try to understand me
Just leave me be.

~

Bad girl, what did you do?
To make your mother reject you?
She doesn't want you, don't you understand?
Don't ask her for a hug or try to hold her hand
She wants a good girl and you are not
Mamma's obviously disappointed with the little girl she got.

~

STATISTICS
Don't turn away from me
I need you, do you not see?
I am crying and I feel so bare
I hate myself but you don't care
My body is aching, marked and bruised
Like the inside of me only that I did not choose
I need you but you are not around
I need your love but there is none to be found
Don't lie to me, only speak the truth
I am more than a statistic of today's abused youth
If there is no truth in what you say
Don't mislead me with false hope, just stay away
Please I beg of you not to hurt me any more
I am knocking on death's door
But I do not want to join the number
Who have gone too soon before.

~

OBLIVIOUS
How wonderful to be as oblivious as you
Oblivious to everything he did to me, all I went through

This Tangled Web

What a luxury for you to decide I am okay now
To never have known the true extent of it all anyhow
How lovely for you to be able to say 'it is history'
Yet it lives on year after year inside the core of me
Oh to be blissfully unaware as you are of the nightmare
Turn your head to face it and it is still right there
But you have decided to leave it all behind
I cannot leave my little girl in your oblivious mind.
~
What have I done to be in disgrace?
What have I done to leave this place?
He abused me time after time
Yet I am being punished for his crime
I am guilty of making them feel uncomfortable
I am guilty of breaking the no talk rule
Worst of all guilty of being too young to take control
Will they ever give me parole?
~

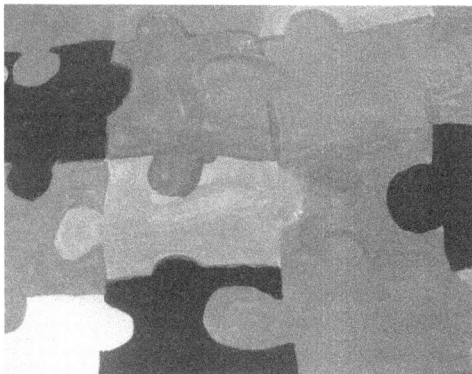

~
You could have hugged me when you knew
Instead you showered me with questions to satisfy you
You could have told me how you felt without ridicule and
shame
Told me you loved me just the same
You could have asked me how it was for me

Dared to look at what you did not want to see
You could have done things differently for my sake
Recognised my agony, responded to my heartache
You could have kept me at home with you
& been strong for me, I did not know what to do
You could have...should have...didn't.

~

I needed you when he laid his hands on my skin
I needed you when I agonised about a life within
I needed you when the police and social workers came
I needed you when I cast my eyes to the floor in shame
I needed you for meetings and decisions, things I didn't understand
I needed you in the dark of night to hold my hand
I needed you, oh mamma how I needed you.

~

THE COST OF PRETENCE
I long to restore all the pieces in place
Yet I know there are some I can never replace
For the child I was has grown and gone
Apart from the memories living on
& of all that it has made me feel inside
Of how they turned away from my cries
I can never fully erase the memory of him
For you cannot purchase new skin
He invaded what you have to keep
Where you think and feel and sleep
The effort of having to smile at you
When my heart is so blue
Of having to be strong
So you can all pretend nothing was ever wrong
It has made my soul sicker than I'd ever dare tell...
Because you have never wanted to reach me in abusive hell.

~

So many things you don't understand, you will never know what it did to me

This Tangled Web

You were never with me in the dark night of my soul and
I never wanted you to be
When I wept alone in the dark and silence of the night
When I sat for hours watching the dark become daylight
When I lay in bed and wondered how I was going to
face another day
When my heart felt like everything it lived for was
snatched away
When I cried and cried and felt I'd never stop it all
When I walked on the edge of life and thought I was
going to fall
When I couldn't look in your face because of the shame
When family passed by in the street like they didn't
know my name
When tablets in my hand and razors by the bed
comforted me enough
To hang on a little longer knowing I had them if it was all
too tough
So many things you don't understand, you will NEVER
know what it did to me.
~
Come and collect your little girl from this place
She lingers in the shadows with invisible tears on her
face
Take her hand, she only wants you
You brought her into this world with a blood red heart
and
allowed others to turn it blue
You gave birth to an innocent child, she was perfect
You failure as parents became her defect
You brought her into this world and then left her alone
You banished her from your heart and home
You fed her to the wolves; you hung her out to dry
You were told she was abused, you called it a lie
& you looked at her with eyes ice cold
& within that look so much was silently told

You had something so precious, so much potential
Then you found her on the edge and watched her fall
I was not born with this despair in my heart
I was born complete, now I feel blown apart
I was born precious, untouched, untarnished
Why, why did you create me for this?

~

The music inside of me plays out of tune since that day
That day when you chose for me to go away
You had carried me inside you for nine months long
You were my everything and your love for me was strong
& then that day when I became torn apart from you
Knowing I could never repair the damage, nothing I could do
Because I had fallen from your grace
What was gone I could never replace
I had slipped too far from your approval of me
Pain and anger in your eyes was all I could see
Nothing for me within your gaze
No feelings of warmth beyond the glaze
No arms to hold me any more
To me you were a slammed and bolted door
My world was never going to be the same
I was numb with pain
& the music continues to play out of tune since that day
As I have waited for you to say the things I doubt you will ever say.

~

Did you see her face when she knew what you had done?
Did you feel any emotion, mine were numb
What could you say, what did you say?
Did she cry after she sent me away?
She kept you close in her care
I went to hell and back, have you been there?
I went and banged on suicide's door

This Tangled Web

& I have done several times more
You lied and played the injured one
You remained her precious son
I was a child and you treated me like a rag doll
Will I ever be able to feel whole?
But did you...did you see her face when she knew?
My heart was breaking in two
I could not look anyone in the eye
Yet it was your damage, your wrong, your lie.

~

Go child, go whilst you can
If not you will wish you had walked away
A few months more and you will wish you had run
What is the sum of this debt you feel you must pay?
For you still pay the cost
In the form of innocence forever lost
Go child, go whilst you can
Go from the place where you were raped
Go from the place of condemnation
Go from where you dare not be yourself
Go from the source of pain and fear
Go to a new place where you can flourish
Go child, go whilst you can...
If not you will wish you had run.

~

My name is tarnished, is guilty, is shame
Because he placed his hands on me, I will never be the
same
His hands that grabbed and touched and held me tight
Did things no one can ever make right
& Mummy said I was a bad girl...bad
Told me she could not hug me, I knew I had made her
sad
Couldn't hug me because I am no good
Though I tried to stop it, I never could.

~

Why do you remain silent when I need you to speak?
Why do you withdraw your help from me when I feel so weak?
Come on have some courage to tell it out
I need to, that is why I cry & scream & shout
Tell me what you are thinking and how you feel
Why do you turn your back on me when I feel so ill?
I have hurt myself on the wall of your silence repeatedly
Is it that you think so damn little of me?
How can your heart collude with this silent carry on?
Is there nothing you want to say to me before I am gone?

~

One final sentence, one final thing...
"She killed herself last night"
One final act to put everything right
One act to say all I cannot say, my reply
One final answer to all the pain you make me feel
All the tears you cause me to cry
One less person to be a pawn in your game
One less, I don't have to remain
One last time to think of me
One last time and then all are free
One last attempt for you to hear how much I wanted you
One less hoop to jump through
One final thing, one final sentence
"She killed herself last night"
One final thing to make everything right.

~

CHAPTER 4...INNER CHILD

She is innocence through and through...

One of my biggest struggles in therapy was learning to listen to and accept my inner child. I remember hating her and not wanting to even look at her. It took a long time for my feelings towards her to begin to change, but you can see in my writing the battle I had. I do think looking back it was a massive part of getting better...accepting her and learning to nurture her. I can still have negative thoughts about her but now I have another insight and I can re-balance my thinking. It really, really was tough though! The 3 hardest things of therapy were...being able to even speak about things...finding my inner child...realising I was never going to have what I wanted from certain relationships I held very tightly to. Everyone has an inner child whether he or she is wounded or healthy.

Can I give to you my badness; will you take it away from me?
Will you explain to the little girl that she can go free?
Can I tell you what happened without looking at the floor?
On those well guarded secrets can I open the door?
Can you help the little girl to see who is really bad?
Hold her in your arms when she is feeling sad
Can you take her to a safer place?
Will you look her in the face?
You must believe in her and tell her she isn't to blame
Tell the bad girl she is good and begin to dissolve the shame.

~

REFLECTIONS

To look into your face, to look into your eyes
To see what he did to you and to realise
That you were just an innocent, powerless kid
To think about what he put you through, the things he did
To look into your face, to look deep inside of me
I'm scared of what is inside and I do not wish to see
Because I am terrified, terrified of who I really am
Terrified it will never change, trying to believe it can
To look into your face and see your hurt and fear
To recall your thumping heart whenever he came near
To think about how he violated you and the physical pain
To think about judging eyes and the sting of shame
You see what it means to look her in the eye
I know I need to embrace her but can only cry
I know she is relying on me to pull her through
Tell me though I feel so helpless...tell me what I can do?

~

MY CHILD/MY ENEMY

I weep for her, I weep for my little girl today
For the freedom and innocence she had taken away

This Tangled Web

I want to embrace her and yet struggle so much to do so
For she is not quite the little girl I wanted to know
Yet the two of us fight to live all in one being
I know from my captivity she needs and deserves
freeing
I dare not look her in the eye because pain stares back
at me
All that he did to her, I do not wish to see
Yet I cannot leave her all alone, she is so young
She looks at me wide eyed and asks me what she has
done
How can I be angry with one so young and small?
Oh help me please to rescue my child from such a
painful fall.

~

~

I listen to the child inside
Day and night she cries
Tell her she is cherished within your heart
She is so torn apart
Love her just because you do
Not for anything she can be for you
Set my tortured soul free
Won't you speak those words to me?

~

The truth is I am so angry; I don't even want to look at you
Or to accept you even exist and are a part of me too
You make me feel so rubbish deep within
You remind me of the past, you remind me of him
If I could cut you away from me then I would
I want to silence you, if only I could
You were not the child you were supposed to be
You are an aching reminder
A symbol that neither of us are who we wanted to be.

~

ON MOTHERS DAY

On Mothers day I am going to remember you my inner child
I am going to call to mind all the things done to you hurtful and wild
I am going to remember the mother you wanted and needed so bad
To look into your face all terrified, sorrowing and sad
I am going to think about the mother you never knew
The mother who turned her back, rejected and failed you

On Mothers day I am going to remember you my inner child
That babe so precious, so innocent and mild
I am going to remember all that you are despite your pain
The lovely pictures you draw, the games you play, the sunshine in
your face, despite your secret rain
I remember your little hands, little fingers, long flowing hair
I will look at you and see a blameless beautiful child there

This Tangled Web

On Mothers day I am going to mother you
I am going to do whatever it is that you little one choose
to do
I am going to sit alongside you or hold you a while
Let you be real, just let you be in tears or with a smile
Whatever it is that you need
Whatever wound I can tend to stop the bleed

On Mothers day I am going to celebrate the wonder you
are
The journey you have made, you have come so far
I am going to remember your innocence, remember the
babe
I am going to remember all the lovely things you have
made
I am going to be like a mother to you today...
In every possible way.
~
Pick me up off the floor and hold me tightly
Take every trace of him from me
My arms, my arms are hurting so much
& I feel sick inside, soothe away his touch
I cannot look at you; I cannot look into his eyes
Cannot stand to see what is there, myself I despise
He kissed me and I feel so unclean
My head is all mixed up; I don't know what things mean
Terrified, too terrified at times to speak
So tired now, tired and weak
Will it happen again, will you keep me from him?
Can you turn me inside out and wash me clean within?
Can you take away the memory of what he did?
Can you forgive the secret kept hid?
How can you stand to touch me when I feel so filthy
inside?
How can you restore my childhood, for it has slowly
died?

~

Take this emotional disability
Take this chaos raging inside of me
Take this darkness that thunders like a storm
Take my child in from the cold and keep her warm
Take what was yesterday
Take it far away
Take the abuse that never lets me forget
Take the shame and regret
Take my tomorrow
Take the heart full of sorrow
Take away my bad dreams
Take away my hopes now fallen apart at the seams
Take away this feeling
BRING my innocent little girl some healing.

~

I hear you screaming inside of me
I hear you screaming to be free
I know you did not want what happened to you
I will call to account for what you have gone through
I know that you are tired, tired as hell
Tired of hiding within your shell
Little girl I hear you shout
I know what it is all about
I hear the pain and I see it on your face
I know you are scared in this place
Stop it little one...
Stop struggling
Stop holding back the tear
You will not find any condemnation here.

~

Little girl, who is going to love you if I don't?
Who is going to show you acceptance if I won't?
I realise I am the only one on which you can depend
I know you look to me for your battered heart to mend
The only person who truly knows what you endured at
his hand

This Tangled Web

The only person who can totally understand
Little one, you scare me and you sadden me through
and through
Yet all you have is me and all I have is you.

~

My heart is walking in the wilderness
Passing through memories, dreams, flashbacks
Was I really born for this?
Walking this place so barren and stark
Even the morning here seems so dark
I can hear nothing but the sound of breaking
As my heart is ripping, splitting, aching
I run to every corner of this place
Mine is the only face
My feet are bare and bleeding, worn almost to the bone
I look up but the sky holds no stars, I am truly alone
I search for a friend, I search for some relief
In searching I find myself cold, tired and awash with
grief

I walk on a little further and there I find a grave
My inner child is buried there, no longer fighting and
brave
She lies forgotten in the ground, gone is her day
Gone is her moment to be a child again, to play
I fall down on my knees and weep bitter tears
For her stolen innocence and lack of years
The earth is cold, dusty and dry
Only silence meets my screams of why
Once more I rise to walk the wilderness
Passing through memories, dreams and flashbacks
Yes...I think I was born for this.

~

I want to rid myself of you
For the things you have done and continue to do
Why were you born, you wretched being
I cannot have compassion for the way you are feeling
You did it, nobody else
Now you are scared to take a look at yourself
People will tire of your moods and tears
Are you going to stay like it for years?
Why don't you cease to be?
Go on, set me free
You are a horrid little girl
Stop twisting my world
I do not want to look at your face
Yet you are within me at every place.

~

Anger flowing through me, threatening to spill out
Needing to be angry, to scream and shout
Tell me how to spend this energy
This power, this force, this poison bubbling in me
So angry and yet so hurt too
So furious and yet so calm with you
Like a wounded animal lashing out because it is
suffering
A wounded child lashing out because of HIM

This Tangled Web

Anger, so much anger, more than I can show
More than I would want to know
Destroying him...no, destroying my child
That anger is driving me wild.
~
She was innocent, she was complete
She was whole, she was a child sweet
She was forced, she was manipulated
She was abused, she was ill fated
She was innocent, she was complete
She was whole, she was a child sweet
She was held down, she was his toy
She was hurt, she had to endure for him to enjoy
She was innocent, she was complete
She was whole, she was a child sweet
She was blamed, she was rejected
She was emotionally neglected
Was she innocent?
She was
Was she complete?
She was
Was she whole?
She was
Was she a child sweet?
She was.
~
Grown
Adult
Independent
Responsibilities
Do for self
Get for self
Make for self
Be strong
Be capable
Little

Kate Swift

Girl
Inside
Weak
Lonely
Crying
Abandoned
Alone
Over and over.

~

THE LITTLE GIRL WHO WALKS IN SHADOWS
You are bad and will always be that way
You are bad and nothing can take that away
Bad to the core, been bad for years
It cannot be made good or washed away with tears
Even Mamma said you were bad when you were small
Bad though you did no wrong, bad though you broke no
rule
Nobody will want you when you are that bad inside
Little girl, it is best that you continue to hide
I know you did not mean to get it all so wrong
But in the shadows of shame is where you belong
I cannot rescue you from the past
I cannot take away the dark shadows it has cast
Rotten to the bone and yet wanting to be redeemed
Walking in the shadows waiting for her soul to be
cleaned.

~

Turn on the light inside her soul
Embrace the hurt and make her whole
If only you knew how much she needs you today
Your little girl is slipping away
Slipping into adulthood...
Carrying all those twisted emotions you never
understood.

~

She is my baby and you took away her innocence

This Tangled Web

*You abused her and smiled through a sickening
pretence
She is my baby and I cry for her at night
I see where she hurts, where you held her too tight
She is my baby and you used her, left her on the floor
You took everything and still came back for more
She was my baby and you stole her away
& you left in her place a terrified raped child that day.*

~

*Little girl go play with your toys, it will be okay
I have made the bad man go away
Little girl come hug me if you are feeling blue
The bad man should never have done that to you
Little girl you are safe, he cannot hurt you any more
I yelled and screamed at the bad man, pushed him out
the door
Little girl I wait to hear your laughter again
The bad man should be the one in pain
Little girl, you are MY little girl, you are precious to me
Bad man deserves to be cold and lonely
Little girl, go live in your little girl's world and know you
are safe
This is your time and this is your place.*

~

*I betrayed my child today
She needed me and I walked away
The child inside screamed to be listened to
But I found so many other things to do
I smiled whilst inside she cried out in pain
I shut her away, didn't want her to affect me again
She begged me not to leave her all alone with only her
memory
But I turned and walked, trying to wriggle free
She wanted a hug, needed some of my time
Yet I told her the day was mine
But one day she will have to be released*

One day she will have no need to scream at me
When all our pain has ceased.

~

IN DEEP
Do you know how much remembering hurts me?
Do you know how I long to be free?
I want it so much because it hurts real bad
The little girl inside me makes me feel so sad
I get to the point where I don't know what to do
I don't want to listen any more to what she has been
through
I want her to be quiet and yet I know she hurts so much
She needs my hugs but is tainted by his touch
All the remembering makes me feel so much pain
She reminds me time and again
I want to cut away the little girl who continues to weep
I want to cut away the memories that go deep
& I am more scared than you will ever know
The fear just seems to grow
The little girl is too much for me, too broken, too in need
How is it I can help her when I too continue to bleed?

~

Give her a chance; give her a chance to thrive
Give her what she needs to do more than just survive
Give her a break, she deserves one from you
Give her loving care, she is hurting too
Tell her that you understand, you know she did her best
Tell her she has nothing to prove to you, let her rest
Tell her you love her and that she matters in your eyes
Tell her you want to hold her when she cries
Take her from her place of pain
Take her into life again
Take her from her shattered past
Take her to a place of peace at last
Hold her and show her you honestly care
Hold her and let her know you are there
Hold her and dissolve her shame and regret

This Tangled Web

Hold her abused body and never forget
Make her the person she was born to be
Make her free
Make her realise she does have worth
Make her glad to be alive, stop cursing her birth
She is a child who was innocent and is innocent still
A child who was captive to his will
A child who did no wrong
A child who in your arms will be strong
You can...heal her
You can...heal her
You can...heal her
YOU ARE HEALING HER.

~

TESTING WHAT IS TRUE
I get so lost for words, tell me what to say
I want to take your pain away
I want to remove the thorn from your child sized heart
So many things are wrong, where shall I start?
Mummy loved you and didn't really mean those things
you heard
You must not own what she said, let go of every
poisonous word
Words said in a moment of anger have bound you up so
long
She called you a bad girl and she was so wrong.

~

When does she get released to go free?
That little kid stamping around inside of me
She screams and wonders why and weeps
Finds no place of rest, no peace in sleep

When does she get told I do love her so?
That she is free to be herself and free to go?
Locked in the darkness, held a prisoner in shame
Frozen by pain

When does she give it all back to him?
& choose not to drown but to turn and swim?
To rise above her chaotic beginning
To defeat him and be able to say she is winning

When does she get accepted, told she is okay
Let out in the light to play?
Embraced, forgiven, restored and made new
Feeling as good as you or you or you

When does she stop feeling robbed of something so
personal?
When can she hold her head high and walk tall?
Told she has rights and has great worth
Made to feel glad for her birth?

~

LITTLE-BIG GIRL
She is there although you cannot see
The little girl inside of me
She tells me I am weak but I am strong
She tells me its abusive hell but I have moved on
She tells me she wants a family but I can stand alone
She tells me she needs someone but I can make it on
my own
Because I will cover my ears when she speaks
& I will cover my eyes when she weeps
I refuse to look back at yesterday
Or she will have got her own way
You cannot see her and I am glad
You cannot see how I am bad
You see the smiles and I dry my own tears
You see the smiles and laughter as I mask the fears
Tell me though, will she always be...
A little girl lost inside of me?

~

Nothing can console the child who weeps bitter tears
Nothing can return to her those stolen years

This Tangled Web

Rip my heart out and let me be at peace
In the field of nightmares there is no release.

~

MY BABE
Oh my babe what is happening to you?
Has someone done you wrong, what did they do?
The roses in your cheeks, I've watched them fade and
die
Now through walls I hear you cry
I want to warm your heart that is encased in ice
For what do you pay this price?
Concern and frustration lingers
You are slipping, like sand through fingers
Oh my babe, are you lost forever?

~

I walk into the room and there she is, my little girl on the
floor
Curled up in the nightshirt which in impatience he tore
Her eyes are cast down to the floor, looking anywhere
but at me
She is locked in a world of fear, I don't know if I can set
her free
Her long brown hair is tangled and twisted, it hides her
face
Shame and silence is all I trace
Her arms are folded, wrapped around her tight
Her body hurts inside and out...
She cannot tell me what he did to her last night.

~

Listen, listen to my scream
Things are not all they seem
I cannot stop screaming for what he did
My precious child, my little kid
Abused, degraded...so young
On her knees for the sins of the son
Listen, listen to my scream.

~

HEAVEN'S CHILD

See the child in heaven playing as happy as can be
That is the little girl inside of me, I have set her free
Her body is perfect now, no longer ill used
She is a good girl and has no memory of being abused
She is what she was meant to be and feeling cherished
Her earthly nightmare has perished
Nothing to hurt her now, nothing to make her afraid
Her heart and soul have been re-made
Be happy sweet innocent one
You can play forever now in the warmth of an eternal
sun.

~

There she was, little hands and feet, long brown hair
At the side of her mother and I watched her standing
there
And my heart ached as tears fell from my face
For she reminded me of her and took me back to that
place.

~

A stupid, worthless, cheap rag doll
Who is broken beyond repair, never again to be whole
On the floor is where he left her when he walked away
Like an old battered toy no longer useful in play
But she is not a rag doll...she is a child...she is mine
You HAVE to listen to her, you HAVE to help her
You HAVE to make her fine
Because you cannot leave her alone on the floor
Because I will not let her be a victim any more.

~

My child does not play
She searches for the things he took away
She lies awake in the middle of the night
In a fear that grips her tight
When she wakes, she thinks of what he did the night
before

This Tangled Web

She is afraid he might do it some more
Paints a smile on her face and walks downstairs
Tries to forget, tries to ignore his stares
My child does not play
Because she was raped yesterday.

~

I am just a child and don't expect more than you can
give
Make friends with me and we can both live
The past is gone and the future waits up ahead
I will be at peace if you help to put the memories to bed
I actually want very little, it is just that I feel so bad
So ashamed, disgusting and sad
I am sorry that I upset you, it makes me upset as well
But I am too small to keep big secrets, I have to tell
Cutting yourself doesn't make me feel safe inside
I don't want you to hate me and force me to hide
If only you could look at me and not despise
If only you could turn your ear to my cries
I am not your enemy
I am you and you are me.

~

MY SURVIVOR'S CREED
1. I will not deny your existence
2. I will not deny your joy and pain
3. I will not ever hold you responsible
4. I will never forgive your abuser
5. I will never wish 'him' any violence as both you and I
hate violence
6. I will create opportunities for you and us to be a child,
to be excited
7. I will honour how you survived by helping others to
survive
8. Whilst I will not forget the abuse, I will strive to move
on from the shadow of it
9. I will speak up when I can

10. *I will not allow what you went through to be minimised*
11. *I will strive to give you what your little heart craves*
12. *I will use the pain you have suffered to release others from theirs.*

~

CHAPTER 5...Depression-On the edge

Being placed in a wilderness to roam...

This chapter includes a lot of poems containing suicidal thoughts and feelings...it is not to glorify the idea of suicide, far from it. It is to help people have an insight into the mind of someone who at the time of writing was suicidal. I hope it will help people who are feeling low to feel that the thoughts they are having are not beyond understanding...and also you can get beyond them. You go beyond them not by taking the ultimate way out but by seeking and sourcing the 'correct' help for you. You do not feel better overnight, it is a long journey and some days I lived moment by moment, contemplating an hour was too much. Live in each single moment and you will find you have done the day. Even after my attempt at taking my life, I was not grateful to still be here...I couldn't understand why I wasn't like the many others who say how grateful they were to have survived...it's taken a long time to feel that sense of gratitude.

Some people say suicide is the 'coward's way out' but for me I was not being cowardly, I was really unwell, too unwell to realise how unwell I was at the time and it was only a while after I started to get better that I realised how different my mind was during that time. I just had to escape from myself. It is still painful to remember the events of that time but important to remember...so I never get back there. If you ever feel like there is nothing left for you...there is...you just haven't found it yet. I also understand now how much the ability to reason is so unbalanced when you get to the point of feeling suicidal. Please see the links page for sources of help if you need it. I was still in my teens when I had my first clinical depression and I remember so clearly sitting in a park for hours...watching people going about the day...and I just kept asking myself "how is it they can function?"..."how is it they can do that?"...That is depression talking...When you are better you will be the person going about your day. I also understand now how much the ability to reason is so unbalanced when you get to the point of feeling suicidal. I only realised when I was getting better just how unwell I had been.

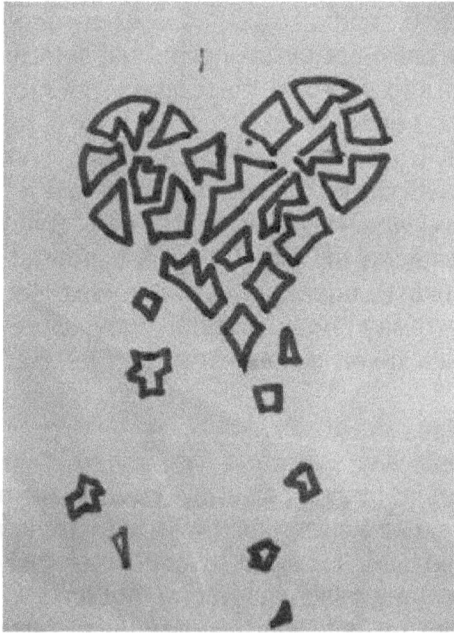

~

Can I slip away?
Can I just drift to sleep for a final day?
If you knew how I felt inside
Would you try to stem the tide?
Of sadness and pain
Tired of feeling this way time and again
If I told you I feel broken in two

This Tangled Web

Would you make me feel less broken, could you?
Can I slip peacefully away tonight?
Whisper peace to me...that everything is all right
What if I said I feel ripped apart?
That pain rules every cavern of my heart?
Tell me there is something better beyond today
Melt all of my chaos away
If I told you I feel so alone in a crowded place
That I long for a reassuring face...
Can I slip away?
~

FLOWERS IN THE DESERT
Tell me there'll be flowers in the desert
Something to pierce the darkness of my deepest hurt
Can something new grow where weeds strangle
everything in sight?
A dawning to cancel out my night
Can flowers grow on barren land?
Can I create anything good from his hand?
Would anything want to grow on the land I have
created?
Or is everything diseased, twisted, dying, suffocated?
~

I cannot express the jumble in my brain
The hectic thoughts a continual drain
The churning feeling deep inside
An uneasy sense of red alert that makes me want to
hide
My legs feel like they are about to drop
My head is busy oh so busy, refusing to stop
Pain down my neck and tension in my shoulders
Little obstacles look like mighty boulders
Body so tired and weary
Eyes staring blankly all teary
Where can I find me?
~

~

I am plummeting in the depths of the dark ocean
Emotionally drowning in slow motion
Lungs filling up with despair like in times gone by
How do I breathe whilst I sob and cry?
Who can rescue me now the rescuers leave one by
one?
Where is the surface, where is the sun?
Where is my shoreline, where is my safety net?
I have not seen hope yet
I'm way down in the depths of the deep
Where one can only sigh and weep.

~

Where do you go when your heart aches in a way no
doctor will understand?
Where do you go when you need to be alone and yet
want to hold a hand?
Where do you go when the silence is too silent but the
noise in your mind drones on?
Where do you go when you want to fall to pieces and
not be told to be strong?
Where do you go when the winter in your soul seems to
have no end?

This Tangled Web

Where do I go?
Please tell me where I go
Where do I go now the winter in my soul seems to have
no end?
~
I am scared
Scared of who I am today
Scared of how I am today
Scared of tomorrow
Scared of putting one foot in front of the other
Scared of my aching heart
Scared of just 'being'
Scared of being scared.
~
Been stuck inside this prison so long
I made it myself now I have to be strong
Have to struggle with all of my might
Have to be strong for this fight
But I am so tired, so crushed in spirit
Just about ready to quit
Will I break out of this prison and be a butterfly
Or will I shrivel up and quietly die?
~
Don't know what to do when I feel this way
You have heard already the things I need to say
I just want to be loved, that is all
Intense is the pain and hard is the fall
It hurts so much but I can't make you see
It's not the physical pain that is crushing me
I need someone to take my hand
You have not walked my path, you cannot understand
How the memories invade my dreams
How they make my day fall apart at the seams
I've cried so hard until no more I can take
It hurts too much to stay awake.
~

Can I rest here with you for a while?
Can I borrow a smile?
Need shelter from the rain
Can you help me to carry this pain?
Would you lend me hope? I mislaid mine
Lost in the chaos of time
Can I share your light? Mine has gone out
Will you remind me once more what life is about?
Can I rest here with you today?
I seem to have really lost my way.

~

My mind is like a stormy sea
My thoughts crashing back and forth like waves
There is no peace
My mind is like a whirlwind
Spinning round and round, making me dizzy
There is no peace
My mind is like a tornado
Destroying and unsettling all in its path
There is no peace
My mind is like a car in the dark with no headlights
Not knowing which way to turn next
There is no peace
My mind is like the sky before sunrise
Waiting for the light to illuminate the darkness
& peace to rise again.

~

This Tangled Web

~

Rushing
Almost colliding
Jolting
Too much activity
Gathering speed
Building into a crescendo that never comes
Chaotic and yet kind of numb
So by
Never slowing
Dangerous
A runaway train
This is the state of my mind
Such an exhausting drain.

~

BROKEN PIECES
Tonight I looked at the cup on the floor
Smashed, cracked, shattered, broken and of no use any
more
In that cup I saw myself, the way in which I feel inside
Smashed, cracked, shattered, broken
I cradled that cup within my hands and I cried.

~

Cried so hard I thought I would choke

*Coughing so hard as if my lungs were full of thick black
smoke
Sobbing into the darkness, drowning in agony
Heart feels like someone has fiercely punched me
Punched me right in the chest, taking my breath away
I am choking on life this very day.*

~

~

*Feeling totally desolate tonight
A wasteland in my soul with no nourishment or light
An aching feeling that eats away and eats away
That does not allow for rest or play
No words can cover the intensity of my pain
Like high winds and lashing rain
I feel soaked, soaked to the core
Drenched in pain, how much more?
Desolate tonight
No nourishment or light.*

~

*So easily
So very easily
So simple
So plain
Beckons the answer
So easily
So very easily
So plain
Beckons the answer...*

This Tangled Web

To my pain.

~

Bits and pieces...
Are my head and all that is mine?
Bits and pieces...
Is where I am today?
Bits and pieces...
Have drifted away
Bits and pieces...
That is my heart after a knife
Bits and pieces...
That is my heart and that is my life.

~

Feelings as fierce as fire burning in my soul
Screaming that I will never be good enough, never be
whole
Good times fade fast and mistakes are on repeat
& hope lays dead...dead at my feet.

~

I reach up but there is nobody to catch my hand
The ground beneath my feet feels like sinking sand
Choked with pain bubbling inside
Looking for a shelter in which to hide
No arms to hold me or catch me should I fall
Little girl all grown up, feeling so scared and so small.

~

I look but I despise what I see
Don't like the reflection staring back at me
So many imperfections, so many things to regret
So many memories I would rather forget
A body clumsy, ugly and longing to be thin inside
So many aspects of me I need to hide
Who is this person staring back at me?
She is so far removed from who I want her to be.

~

Tell me why I must wait for a new day

Tell me why I have to stay
Tell me it will be worth it in the end
Tell me the road is straight after this bend
Tell me why wait for tomorrow at all
Catch me...no, do not catch me...please let me fall.
~
I want to die because you did those things to me
I want to die because I know I will never be free
I want you to know the way I feel
This is not a game, this is for real
I want to take myself away
So I don't have to face this one more day.
~

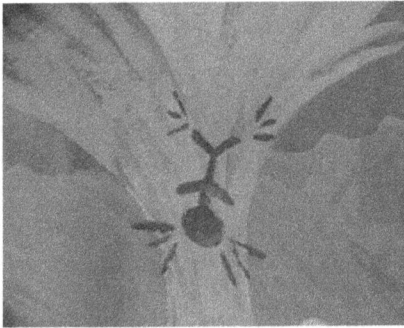

~
Things feel wrong somehow today
I want to curl up tight and hide away
If I step towards the feeling, tears begin to well
Hide me; keep me in a hard shell
Away from this world with its pressures and pain
Away from myself, mind feeling chaotic again
Things feel wrong today although I look all right
Tired from a troubled sleep, a lonely night
Smiling at you but inside I want to cry
Feel like I could scream but I don't know why
I feel like I am looking for myself, lost in a haze
Going round in circles, going stir crazy in this maze.
~

This Tangled Web

Who flicked off the light?
Turning my world to constant night?
People speak of good things for me
Yet I cannot see
All is dark inside my head
Hope lays dead.
~
Take it
Have it
I don't want it
Take it back
Listen to me
I don't want it
I don't want this damn life
~
So easily, so easily
Those tablets could take me
Easy to take, hard to resist
I resent being born for this
The torment of those pills
The answer to my ills
Could I really be free...so easily?
~
Not today and not tomorrow
I'm done, I'm feeling so hollow
Nothing to hold on for, I think I will let go
Today...tomorrow...NO
~
How is it that you can see hope for me?
I think I am useless, a nothing, so unworthy
I see nothing in tomorrow
But the reflection of yesterday's sorrow
I do not want to live on
I feel so weak and yet you see me as strong
I have no desire to get better, no desire at all
I want to die, I want to fall

How do you see potential in a mistake such as I?
Why can't you understand my desire to die?
Why do you have time for me and place in me some worth?
I curse this day and I curse my birth
Tablets to make me well again
I don't want them; I want to escape this pain
Do not speak of hope to me, I don't want any hope
To take myself away from here is the only way I can cope
But you show me kindness; you try to show me a different reality
How is it that you can see hope for me?

~

I think I would rather be a firework soaring into the air
Out of the deep dark ground without effort or care
Into the night sky, bursting forth into beauty
A sparkling, dazzling moment, everyone admiring me
Then to dust without time to fear or feel a thing
Yes I'd rather be a firework...
beauty
wonder
awe
light
For a moment I would bring
Then to the ground, no more expectation to perform
As I lay in an unknown place going cold but feeling warm.

~

Nothing matters any more
Nothing can get me
No one can leave me
Nothing matters any more
Nothing can hurt me
No one can crush me
Nothing matters any more
Nothing is greater

This Tangled Web

No one can stop me
Nothing matters any more
Nothing can make me lose
Nothing can make me win
Nothing matters any more
I am heading for the exit
I am finding the final door
Because...
Nothing really matters any more.

~

Stupid Life
You make me so sad
Crazy life
You make me so mad
I hate what you do
All the things you put me through
Curse you life and curse this damn day
I don't want to live this way.

~

WEATHER WARNING
On the exterior she is calm and okay
Inside a hurricane is building day by day
Waiting to destroy anything in its path and more
Yet on the exterior all is calm but inside she
just cannot take any more.

~

Acute pain taking my breath away
As my heart dies another death
Lonely tears fall like rain down the window
Feeling so wretched, so broken and low
Comfort is writing a note to say goodbye
Comfort is thinking what it would mean to die.

~

She sleeps...
Now she sleeps, the pain is gone
Let only the good things live on

No nightmares can haunt
No memories can taunt
I've made struggling cease
I yearned and reached out for peace
Now she sleeps and now you know why
Now she sleeps...I love you...goodbye.

~

If life is like a flower, mine has no colour any more
It has no purpose, it is living but I don't know what for
I cannot smell its sweet perfume
The beauty is always gone too soon
Others admire the flower but I do not see what they see
I want to snap the stem, snap the life in me
I despise the flower before my eyes
The thorns cut deeply as the flower slowly dies.

~

This life has got me beat
I can find no place of rest or retreat
Everything feels like too much for me
Inside I feel so empty
Unable to do the things I usually do
Unable to help and please you
Do not ask of me, please do not ask
Living this day seems a great enough task
I am so afraid of this feeling
Somebody show me some healing
Don't ask me about tomorrow, only today
From the edge I am not far away
Feeling tired and alone
Feeling a long, long way from home.

~

Will I?
Shall I?
Can I?
Will I?
Shall I?
Want to...

This Tangled Web

DIE.

~

If I don't sleep I am going to die
All I can do is pray for sleep and cry
Death is so near to me like I could touch it with my hand
I'm talking a language you don't understand
Please God let me sleep.

~

NO GOODBYES
I want to go, don't hold onto me
I know a place where I can be free
Don't make me think of those left behind
Enough pain and chaos in my mind
I long for everything to slip quietly by
With no time to say goodbye.

~

Don't you want to live, to be alive?
To see the sunset and the sunrise
To feel the rain on your face
To discover a new place
To become a parent, a mum
Don't you want to live, dare to believe
To learn some more, to achieve
To watch the children grow up
To drink from life's cup
To see winter turning into spring
To be loved and to be loving
Don't you want to grow old?
To discover things of which you've been told
To walk in the park on a sunny day
To find a new and better way
To see those things you've not yet seen
To wish and wonder, to build a dream
WHY DON'T YOU WANT TO LIVE?

~

The sun was bright the day she died

But she felt torn and twisted inside
The day was hers, full of possibility
But she felt anything but free
Friends told her it would be okay
But she woke each morning and cursed the day
The sun was bright the day she died
She drew her last breath and peace reigned inside.

~

ONE MORE DAY
There is a pain deep inside that will not go away
Can I hold on for one more day?
Take away my heart, it is driving me insane
If only you knew the pain
I need you, oh how I need you to see me
How I need you to free me
I want to cry but the tears do not fall
I scream for you but you cannot hear my call
The pain is so intense, let me lose all feeling
Am I broken beyond healing?
Enshrouded in darkness I cannot find my way
Can I hold on for one more day?

~

I cannot wait in this pain
Feel like I'm drowning again
I can't ignore it, can't push it away
Can't contemplate doing another day
& I wonder what it is like to die
Countless are the tears I cry
I want the world to leave me alone
I want God to take me home
Need to be released
Into the arms of death, arms of peace
Tired of trying
Of pretending, fighting, struggling, crying
Let me go
Life's hell continues to grow
I don't care to be here any more

This Tangled Web

Don't tell me things are worth living for
The demons of the past hold me bound
Maybe no cure can be found
I'm not killing myself to hurt anybody
It's not about them, it's about me
It is totally and unforgivably selfish
But I want this one wish
It's okay for me to go now, it's fine
I'm tired of time
So tired.

~

HAUNTED
By the memories, by the shadows of my life
By the broken dreams and broken promises
By the hand that touched without permission
By the hand that slapped and punched me
By the people whose words burnt into my soul
By the child who never got what she needed most
By the child still lost, still searching
By the man who said he loved me and lied
By the parent who never hugged me
By the mummy who threatened to leave me
By my mistakes
By my failings
By my own shattered dreams
By my failed relationships
By words said in anger
By moments of madness
By times I cannot recall
By the times I can
By who I hoped to be and who I am
I am HAUNTED.

~

CHAPTER 6...SELF HARM

Damaging me to forget about you...

Self harm is a temporary relief from immediate pain but ultimately it is another thing which traps you...it can become habitual and very difficult to stop doing. I have feelings of self harm a handful of times a year now; they have not gone altogether. However, I know it is not a healthy or a helpful way to deal with feelings such as the ones I describe below. I know this now but at the time of writing I was still very much trapped in that web and I coped whichever way I could to make it through the day. I would urge you not to hurt yourself but to find other ways of managing the things which make you want to self harm. For more information and help on self harming please see the links on my website.

This Tangled Web

You comfort me
Comfort as blood I see
You do not hurt as I break the skin
A kind of peace flows within
Release for too many emotions inside
But another scar to hide
Yet you help to numb my pain
You allow me some escape time and again

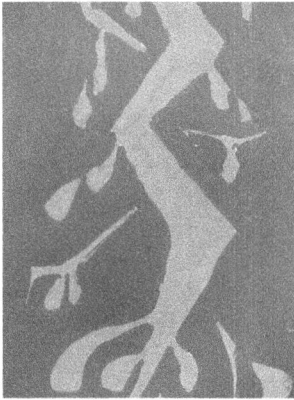

~
I feel no physical pain today
As I make the emotional torment fade away
As my arms become red, I feel nothing but anger inside
As I create yet more scars to hide
I don't care about the damage done to me
Because the harder I hit...the further I push these
emotions away from me.
~
You hurt me so badly
The damage cut so deeply
The physical scars now gone
You would look and say I am strong
But the inner pain flows freely still
You cannot know how I feel

Bad day/good day still feeling low
All the thoughts inside my head
You wouldn't wish to know
Tablets, razor blades...what can I do?
Damaging me to forget about you.

~

~

Pretending nothing is wrong...escaping
Fooling yourself that you're fine...escaping
Cutting to chase away the inner pain...escaping
Pretending that HE does not exist...escaping
Living in the abuse...living after the abuse...
NO WAY OUT
Trapped...how do you escape?

~

I need a razor blade to release the pain
Cannot stand to feel this way again
Need to cut so deep because it hurts more than I can
say
I think about taking myself away
What would it mean to the other me?
How crazy to think I could be free
I hate myself and I see no release
When will this hell cease?

~

You make me so angry; I want to do something stupid

This Tangled Web

To make you stop treating me like a rebellious kid
I want to cut my arms until they bleed and bleed
I don't need you, from you there is nothing I need
Maybe if I took myself away then power would at last be
mine
For you to treat me as you do there would be no more
time
You make me feel so angry within
Why do I have to see him?
I wish I had the courage to swallow lots of pills
To release me from all of our ills.

~

Give me a razor blade, it is what I need
I do not care if I cut and if I bleed
Give me something to escape this feeling
A razor blade is soothing, is healing
I cannot stand to feel this way
I can cut it away
Got to get these feelings out of me
To cut is to remove the pain inside
To restore some sort of peace, to turn the tide.

~

I'm back in this place again
Rage has risen above the pain
I just feel tired and empty now
Once again I fail
Nothing seems that important any more
I have even forgotten what I was so angry for
Looking around I should feel bad
But I am just so sad
I don't even feel what I have done
I want to be alone, yet part of me needs someone
All I have are a few more scars to remind me...
I am still not free.

~

Not a cut but relief from the pain

Kate Swift

Not flowing blood but silent flowing tears
A stinging angry cut
A stung angry heart
It's what I am...ugly
It's mine
I did it
I will probably do it again.

~

Look at my bleeding arms and see
See the pain pouring out of me
See the confusion and bewilderment
The anguish of abandonment
Look at my bleeding arms and see
That I still am not free
Free from him who caused my pain
Free from the memories which remain
Look at my bleeding arms and see
I am not who I long to be
Moments past are etched in my mind
Words that hold you, words that bind
Look at my bleeding arms and see
The pain pouring out of me.

~

If I cut then he has hurt me again
Too many already are the scars of his pain
Yet I feel so many different ways
So much anger remembering childhood days
I don't know what to do with all these things I feel
Need and want to cut
Need and want to heal.

~

Give me a razor blade and leave me alone
I can do what I want, my body is my own
You do not really care what happens to me at all
If I keep on going, stand still or fall
Don't want you to know what I'm doing to me
It is not about you, I am allowed to be free

This Tangled Web

Free from him, free by the movement of the blade
Free from what he did, feel the pain and the memories
fade
Clean up and care for the damage I did
Survive the damage you did to me when I was just a kid.
~
I want a knife
I want to cut
I want to let the pain seep out
I want to cut through it
I want to cut all the badness away
I want to cut all the anger away
I want to cut all the chaos away
I want to see blood
Red and raw
To see it and not to feel it
To no longer feel the pain inside
To feel relief instead
& leave my torture dying and dead.
~
CHAPTER 7...ALL OUR CHILDREN
Open your eyes...

We must turn on the light
Got to pull back the cover of night
We must make ourselves hear
The silent screams of fear
We must make ourselves see
It is our responsibility
See the child who cannot sleep
Who cries too much
Who stares at the floor and resists touch
We must stop the evil claiming our children
Robbing their joy and innocence
Wake up and smell the coffee world
Open your eyes wide and stop the pretence.

~

Children are
Travelers
Seekers
Joy givers
Needing
Searching
Deserving
Children are
Our tomorrow
We must me their needs TODAY.

~

FOR YOU

Just rest in my arms and know for you I am here
There is no need to worry and no need to fear
I will wrap my arms around you
I will shield you from all that is untrue
I will help to restore your broken soul
To touch your life and make it whole
My precious child tell me why tears fall down your face
We can turn your world around
We can make it a wonderful place.

~

I am too young to make myself heard, who will be my
voice?
Who will rescue me from a home life not of my choice?
Who will dare to see it through my eyes, to see what I
see?
Am I worth enough that you will speak up for me?
You don't want to think about my reality but I live it every
day
You could make my life better, show me another way
I am too young to make myself heard, who will be my
voice?
Who will rescue me from a home life not of my choice?

~

THE SILENT CRIMINAL

This Tangled Web

You weave a web of evil, you lie and manipulate
Then you walk away leaving someone full of self hate
You are a cheat to yourself and the worst kind of liar
A power hungry person who does anything to meet his desire
Maybe your excuse is your own abuse when you were young
If that is so, how the hell can you do the same thing to someone?
You trap people; you make them feel like nothing at all
Yes that is you the abuser...the silent criminal.

~

How can you ignore the child who cries?
How can you turn away from the pain in their eyes?
How can you refuse to hear what they need you to know?
How can you fail to see all the signs that show?
The child who needs you cannot reach you
Children are neglected and abused
They would love to be able to turn away from it too
To believe it does not happen but it has repeatedly to them
They spent childhood wishing the abuse would end
Not to talk about it or think about it won't make it go away
It is our problem, yours and mine
Thousands of children are suffering this very day.

CHAPTER 8...BREAKING FREE

After the rain a rainbow my friend...

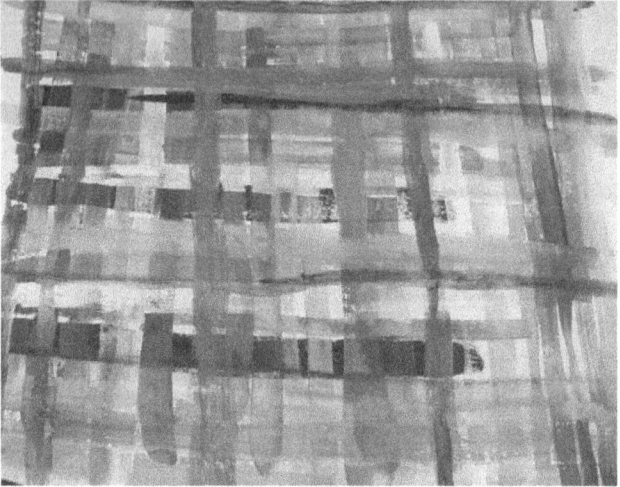

~
~

SURVIVOR STAND STRONG

You stole a piece of our childhood BUT we survived
You made us feel so broken BUT piece by piece we are restored
You made us feel so alone BUT we are many
You made us feel frightened BUT together we are unafraid
You knocked us down BUT we got back up again
You silenced us BUT together our voice is louder than ever
You made us feel bad BUT you were bad
You made us feel ashamed BUT the shame belongs to you
It did not break us and therefore it made us stronger
YES we SURVIVED

This Tangled Web

(Inspired by all the beautiful survivors I have met)

~

JOURNEY OF WHY
For what purpose am I here is the question my soul doth cry
Why this, why that, why then, why, why, why?
What was I born for, where is the reason?
What is this journey, this time and season?
As we travel through this thing called life with its sweet and bitter tears
Some days we can be found on the mountain top flying through our dreams
Tomorrow you may find me weeping, falling apart at the seams
What difference can one person really make in this thing we call living?
The joy in my journey is in loving and laughing and giving.

~

Gradually she decided to take control and lift the lid herself
She went and took that box from the shelf
The contents she emptied all over the floor
One by one she explored them until they held no power any more
With help she looked at the things which had hurt her very much
She remembered the damage, the agony of his touch
Sometimes she cried and wanted to throw it all back in the box
But she had moved on from secrets that chained the soul with
big locks.

~

You cannot hurt her any more

Kate Swift

You are staying behind a locked and bolted door
I am taking back the child you stole
I am working hard to make her whole
She was innocent, you are to blame
You have the guilt and you carry the shame
My little girl was violated
No longer is she to be hated
I am taking the power away from you
I am the strong one now and little me too.

~

I am putting it in its rightful place; I am giving it to him
All the brokenness and shame of his filthy ugly sin
I am putting it at his feet; I am ramming it down his throat
All the things he did to her that made her choke
I'm telling him he was bad and giving my little one some peace
The shackles belong to him and she deserves release
I am telling him he is disgusting, no greater than a piece of dirt
Bringing him to answer and to suffer for my little one's hurt.

~

Screaming and shouting gone
Nothing but a memory to dwell upon
Blame and secrecy blown away
I am heading for my healing day
Lies brought out into the light
No more to haunt me in the still of the night
Childhood memories distanced from me
I am going to a place where I can be free
Tormenting voices silenced
No more twisted stories or violence
I have done it; I have begun to break the chain
& I am never going back again.

~

This Tangled Web

I believe one day I will be free from the shadow of what
you did
From the burden of a secret no longer hid
That I will look at the past and feel okay inside
& fetch from within the child who has wanted to hide
That she will be free to be a child again
That she will laugh more times than she has felt pain
I believe one day I will shed this clumsy figure you see
& everything that is ugly
It might take some time but that day will come
& when it does...
You will still have to live with what you've done.

~

Why face the world this morning?
Because the promise of a new day is dawning
Because those whom you love want you in their day
The clock still ticks and things to be done won't go away
Because if you stay in bed you save it all up for
tomorrow
Then harder the task and more hopeless the sorrow
Live it for someone else if you don't want to live it for
you
Press on in the darkness; press on until the light comes
shining through.

~

HOPE
I am hoping this is the darkest night before a most
beautiful dawn
I am hoping that out of the void something wonderful is
born
I am hoping the silence is going to be filled with laughter
and positivity
I am hoping after walking these corridors one will lead
me to be free
I am hoping for all the tears I cry now, a river of joy
overflows not too far away

*I am hoping the loneliest night will take me on to the
richest day
I am hoping the struggle is worth it, hoping there is
something worth finding
I am hoping against hope tonight because the pain is
blinding.*

~

*Little girl, turn away from your desert of tears
All those storm ravaged and bitter years
Nothing to see in your desert for pleasure
Just agony stretching beyond measure
So turn away from your desert and see
A bountiful land being cultivated just for thee
Know that you can live again
Feeling peace where once was pain.*

~

*PRISONER NO MORE
I rescue the little girl from his hand
I hold her and hug her, try to make her understand
That it is him I am angry with, angry as hell
I know she is too scared and too ashamed to tell
I know that she needs me now more than anything
Into her world some peace I can bring
I am holding her close to me and she is weeping
I am watching over her as she is sleeping
Any questions she has I will try to answer them all
I will be right beside her before and after school
She worries that she is bad and I do not love her any
more
But she has nothing to be guilty for
I just look at her little arms, legs, face
& I know my love can reach her in any place
As for him he has no part of her or me
I will never forgive and he should never be free
Because if I forgave I betray her pain
I would be letting her down again
It takes many words to make her understand why*

This Tangled Web

Why nobody came to rescue her in the night
But I am rescuing her now; I am trying to make it right
I will do anything to restore to her those years she lost
Because she must be free to live her life
& HE must pay the cost.

~

Get down on your knees and tell her what you did was bad
Look her in the eye, that little girl you made feel guilty and sad
Get down on your knees before the world and tell out what you did to that little one
The snatching of innocence and joy that had not long begun
Get down on your knees, look inside yourself and weep
For the little girl you raped when she was trying to sleep
Get down on your knees so she can stand tall and unashamed
For you are accountable, you are rightfully to blame.

~

Little girl, come out from hiding yourself away
Come and meet this new and healing day
Show me where it hurts so I can heal the pain
Raise you up to life again.

~

I AM A SURVIVOR
You pushed me down so many times but I got back up again
You pushed me to the edge of my existence but I worked through the pain
You pushed me aside like a piece of rubbish but I know I am worth more
You pushed me to the ground but I did not remain on that floor
You made me question everything I ever knew
Yet the only questionable thing in my life was you

Kate Swift

You pushed my childhood into a living hell
But I lived to tell because...
I AM A SURVIVOR!

CHAPTER 9...MY SURVIVOR ART

The out workings of inner pain...

Here is almost all of my survivor art as I like to call it. It sounds a bit over-dramatic, but I have said before that when I wrote a lot of the poetry it was pain pushing the pen across the page. The same for much of the art work here, it really is the out-workings of a chaotic or hurting mind. A lot of the pieces were done in art therapy. Art therapy was hard but good for me; it was a really nice medium to work with. With the clay I just found myself making all these figures, usually on my really worst days! Some people are quite disturbed by them not having faces...I don't like putting faces on anything. They are not about artistic merit; if they were we wouldn't get very far! They are for you to make of them what you will...

This Tangled Web

Kate Swift

This Tangled Web

This Tangled Web

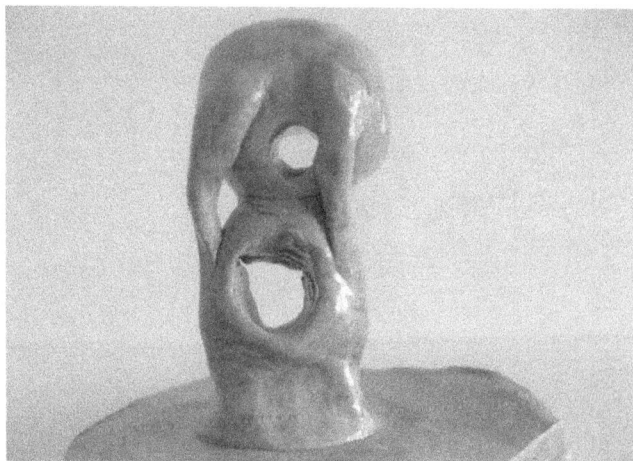

This Tangled Web

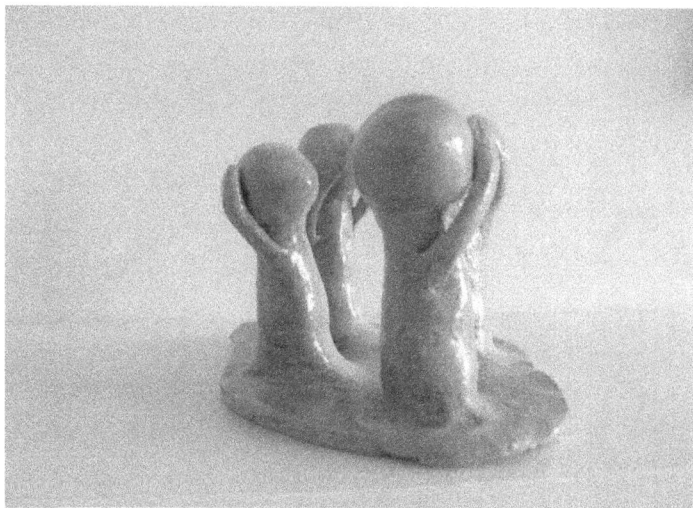

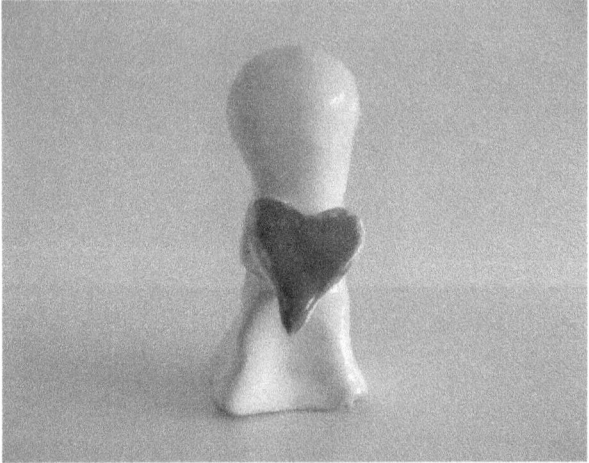

This Tangled Web

This Tangled Web

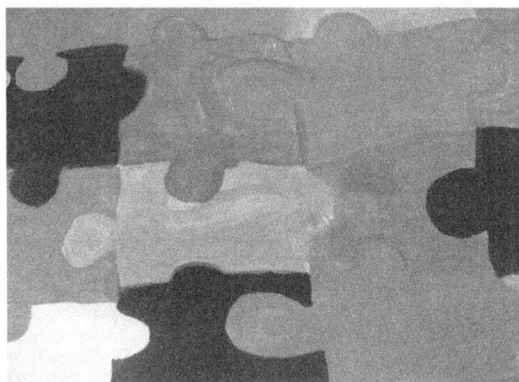

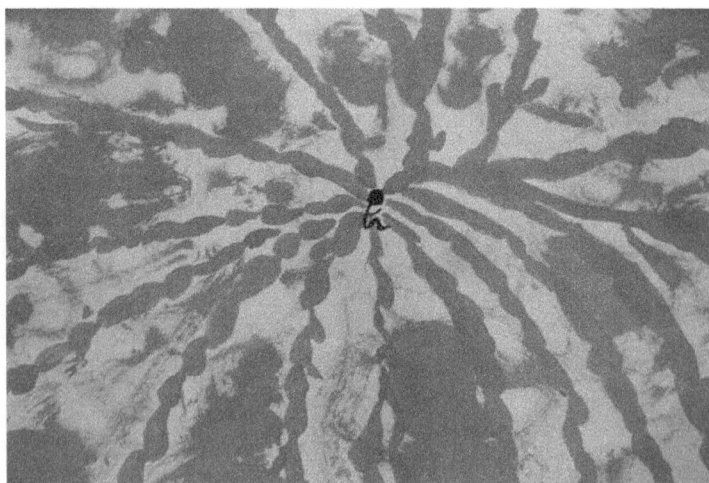

This Tangled Web

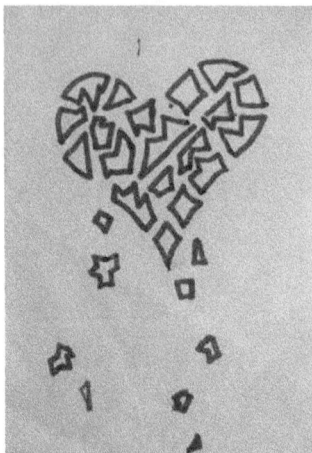

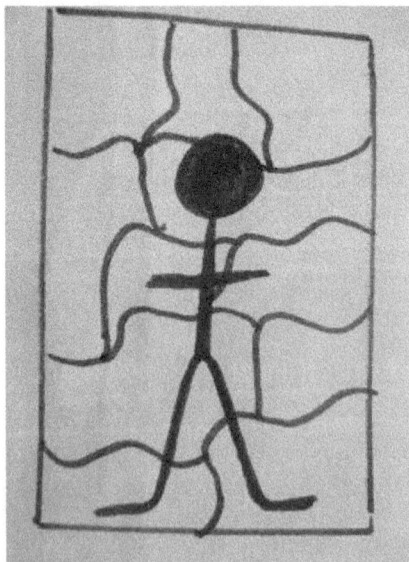

This Tangled Web

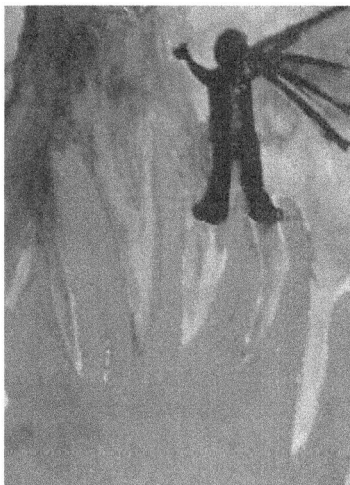

This Tangled Web

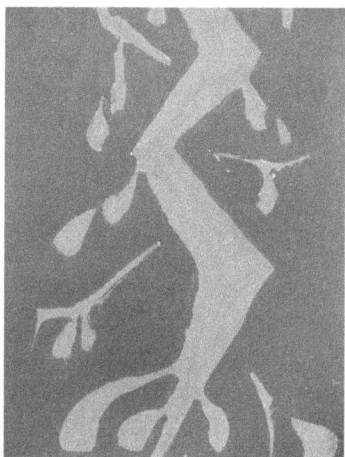

HOW TO CONTACT THE AUTHOR....

You can contact the author via the website www.thistangledweb.co.uk or you can also join us at 'Reaching Survivors of sexual abuse' on Face Book. For further sources of help and information please see the website.